GULF

BUSINESS JULY

2015

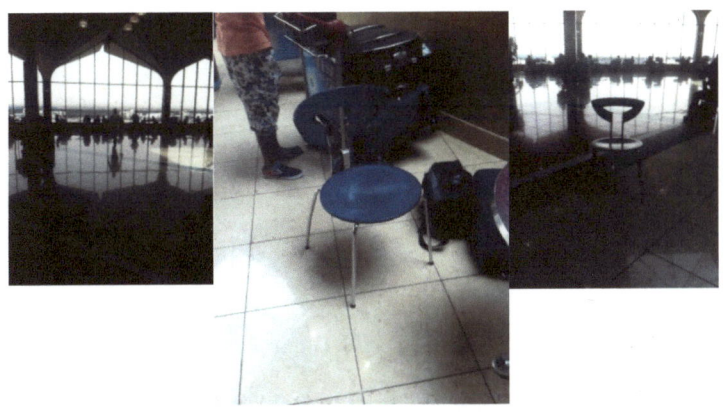

WHATS WRONG WITH DUBAI AIRPORT

ISBN-13: 978-1514684726 FOR FREE COLOURED ONE PAGE ADVERTISEMENTS E MAIL US ON Transoxiana@mail.com
ISBN-10: 1514684721

DAMAC WORLDS

BEST INVESTMENT

GULF NEWS IS A WEEKLY JOURNAL PUBLISHED IN HARD COPY FORM AND DISTRIBUTED TO SUBSCRIBERS AND SOLD BY AMAZON BOOKS.

YOU CAN PLACE FREE SINGLE PAGE COLOURED ADVERTISEMENT.

TO PLACE AN AD SIMPLY E MAIL US ON:--

Transoxiana@mail.com

MULTIPLE PAGE ADS COST 100 USD PER PAGE

Editor in Chief

AGHA H AMIN

Gulf Business

GULF

BUSINESS

VOLUME ONE

1 July- 7 July

Weekly publication to project companies and generate business.

6" x 9" (15.24 x 22.86 cm)

ISBN-13: 978-1514684726 FOR FREE COLOURED ONE PAGE
ADVERTISEMENTS E MAIL US ON Transoxiana@mail.com
ISBN-10: 1514684721

Full Color on White paper

ISBN-13: 978-1514684726

ISBN-10: 1514684721

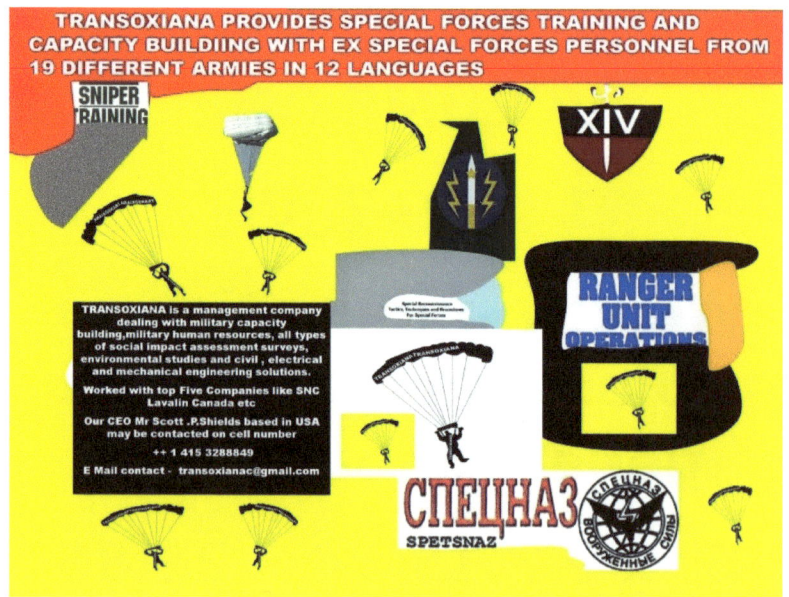

ISBN-13: 978-1514684726 FOR FREE COLOURED ONE PAGE ADVERTISEMENTS E MAIL US ON Transoxiana@mail.com
ISBN-10: 1514684721

ISBN-13: 978-1514684726 FOR FREE COLOURED ONE PAGE ADVERTISEMENTS E MAIL US ON Transoxiana@mail.com
ISBN-10: 1514684721

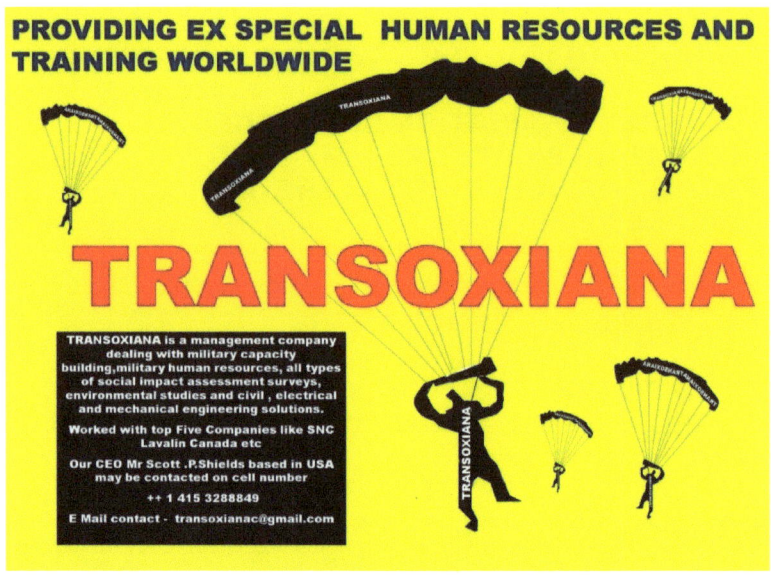

TRANSOXIANA is a management company dealing with military capacity building, military human resources, all types of social impact assessment surveys, environmental studies and civil , electrical and mechanical engineering solutions.

Worked with top Five Companies like SNC Lavalin Canada etc

Our CEO Mr Scott .P.Shields based in USA may be contacted on cell number

++ 1 415 3288849

E Mail contact - transoxianac@gmail.com

ISBN-13: 978-1514684726 FOR FREE COLOURED ONE PAGE ADVERTISEMENTS E MAIL US ON Transoxiana@mail.com
ISBN-10: 1514684721

20'dv CW / 40'dv CW	40'hc CW	
India	Shanghai	Pusan
Nhava Sheva	Dalian	Seoul
Delhi	Tianjin	Inchon
Colombo	Ningbo	Kobe
Calcutta	Qindao	Osaka
Chennai	Xiamen	Nagoya
Cochin	Huangpu	Tokyo
Karachi	Yantian	Yokohama
Chittagong	Shekou	Port Kelang
	Hong Kong	Pasir Gudang
	Kaohsiung	Penang
	Keelung	Singapore
	Taichung	Bangkok
		Laem Chabang
		Jakarta
		Surabaya
		Ho Chi Minh

USED CONTAINERS BOUGHT AND SOLD WORLDWIDE

Transoxiana@mail.com

ISBN-13: 978-1514684726 FOR FREE COLOURED ONE PAGE ADVERTISEMENTS E MAIL US ON Transoxiana@mail.com
ISBN-10: 1514684721

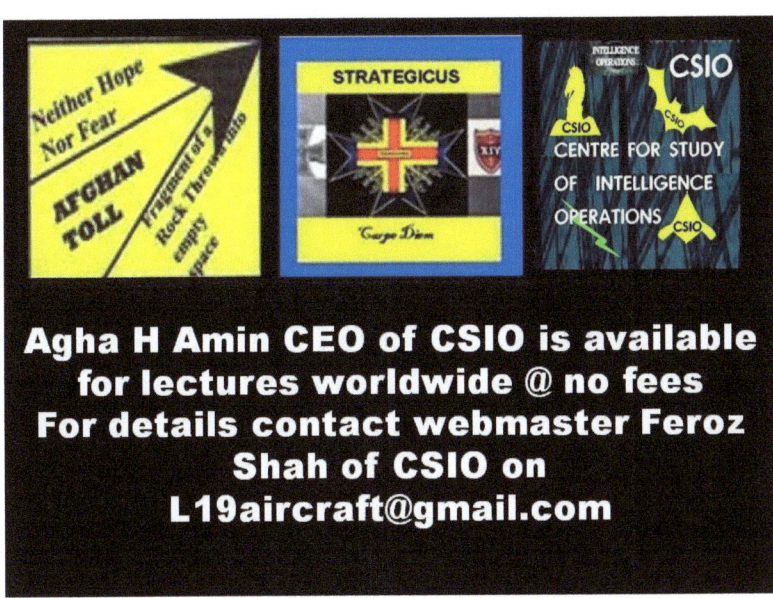

About the Author

Agha H. Amin , Retired Tank corps major who served in five tank regiments and commanded an independent tank squadron and served in various staff , instructional and research assignments. Presently heads think tank Centre for Study of Intelligence Operations. Editor in Chief of monthly Intelligence Review and monthly Military and Security Review.

 In his Pakistan Army tenure he wrote three original tactical papers on Reconnaissance Troops Tactical handling, Reconnaissance support group , and RFS Concept.

 His writings were published in Pakistan Armys prime journals , Pakistan Army Journal and Citadel Journal of Command and Staff College Quetta. His recommendations regarding bifurcation of officer corps into command and staff cadre advanced in 1998 were later accepted.

 In addition his recommendation of grouping various corps into army commands advanced in an article published in Citadel Journal in 1998 were accepted in 2005 or so. Wrote Pakistan Armys first tactical paper on Tactical handling of Reconnaissance Troop in 1986 which is now being incorporated in Pakistan Armys most important general staff publication " The Armored Regiment in Battle". Wrote The Essential Clausewitz in 1993, Sepoy Rebellion of 1857-59 in 1998 , Pakistan

ISBN-13: 978-1514684726 FOR FREE COLOURED ONE PAGE ADVERTISEMENTS E MAIL US ON Transoxiana@mail.com
ISBN-10: 1514684721

Army till 1965 in 1999 ,Development of Taliban Factions in Afghanistan and Pakistan (2010) ,Taliban War in Afghanistan (2009). Served as Assistant Editor of Defence Journal ,Executive Editor of globe and Founder Editor of Journal of Afghanistan Studies .

An associate of the think tanks ORBAT and Alexandrian Defense group. Expert in social impact and environmental assessment carried out various LARP surveys for Asian Bank and World Bank projects.

He has lectured at various think tanks and organisations worldwide and shares his knowledge without any honorarium and at zero financial benefits. Carried out various oil and gas and power transmission line surveys in West Asia. One time Assistant Editor Defence Journal , Executive Editor Globe, Editor Journal of Afghanistan Studies Feedback is welcome at e mail address L19aircraft@gmail.com

ISBN-13: 978-1514684726 FOR FREE COLOURED ONE PAGE ADVERTISEMENTS E MAIL US ON Transoxiana@mail.com
ISBN-10: 1514684721

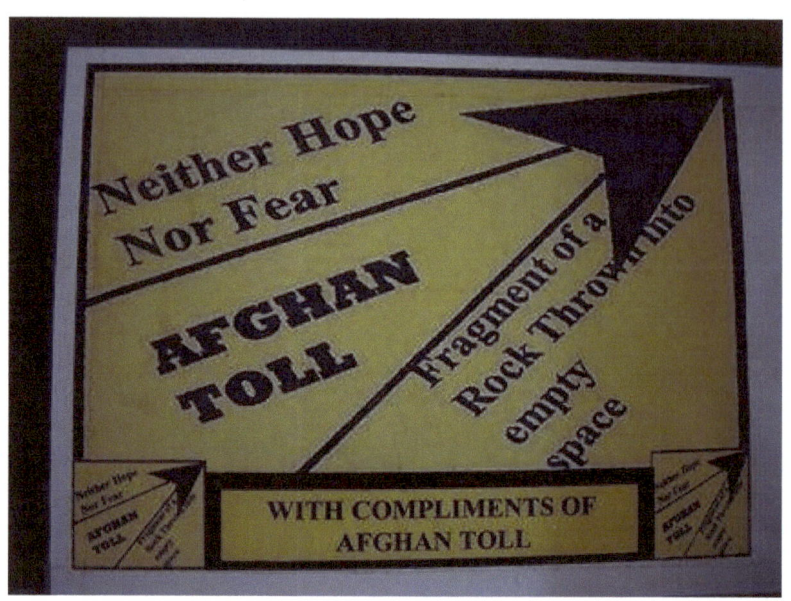

TX OFFERS SUPERIOR AIR DEFENCE AND RADAR CAPACITY BUILDING SERVICES

ELINT Digital Analysis and Exploitation
Analysis process for different objectives(e.g. MTI, rejection performance, integration periods, resolvable range, PRF), data cleaning, data reduction and extraction, signal examination and processing, signal characterisation, interpulse/intrapulse analysis, wideband analysis, pulse doppler analysis, scan analysis, EW analysis, statistical/stability analysis using software tools, e.g. MARTES, ASPEN, search techniques based on airborne/land/ship platforms, PRF selection algorithm.
ELINT Operationalisation
Sensor platforms location considerations, sensor configurations, updating and maintaining emitter and platform databases.

countersurveillance@mail.com
++ 92 333 1327563

PERFORMANCE OF IRAQI AND LIBYAN AIRFORCE AND RADAR SERVICES WAS ZERO IN 1991 , 2003 AND 2011 WARS DESPITE TOP CLASS EQUIPMENT
NO ARAB PILOT EVER SHOT DOWN AN ISRAELI AIR PLANE IN ANY ARAB
ISRAEL WAR. ONLY ISRAELI AIRPLANES SHOT DOWN FLYING. SAME ARAB

ISBN-13: 978-1514684726 FOR FREE COLOURED ONE PAGE ADVERTISEMENTS E MAIL US ON Transoxiana@mail.com
ISBN-10: 1514684721

ELECTRONIC WARFARE CAPACITY BUILDING AT AS LOW AS 100 USD PER DAY

RADAR SPECIALISATIONS

T 13 ,T14 ,P35 RUSSIAN RADAR,CONDOR, AR 1,AR 15,FPS 2O,FPS 6, MPDR,CRC, SECTOR AUTOMATION, HP RADAR KEY STAFF SERVED AS UNIT COMMANDER LOW LEVEL RADARS INCLUDING MPDRS AND CRC.
CRC INCLUDING MPDRS AND ITS INTEGRAL COMMUNICATION.
KEY STAFF SERVED IN MIDDLE EAST AND PARTICIPATED IN NATO EXERCISES/CENTO EXCERICES. TURKISH RADARS, WHERE ELINT EXPOSURE,WAS AVAILABLE,
AMPLE EXPERIENCE TO CONDUCT OPERATIONS UNDER THE JAMMING AND SPOOFING ENVIRONMENTS.
USE OF ECCM WERE EXTENSIVELY EMPLOYED . EXTENSIVE USE OF M.T.I SAW US THROUGH TO OPERATE UNDER ECM ENVIRONMENT.
SPECIALISED EXPOSURE TO ANTI ROTARY OPS IN CONFLICTS RECENTLY AS WELL AS MAZEN DORF STUDY INVOLVING JAMMING ROTARY WING CRAFTS IN WAR ZONES.
KEY STAFF PARTICIPATED IN DETECTING AND DEFEATING 5 MAJOR INTRUSIONS BY WORLDS TOP AIRFORCE IN BATTLE ENVIRONMENT.
TEAM INCLUDES NATO, RUSSIAN , CHINESE , KOREAN , IRAQI,LIBYAN AND ISRAELI EX DEFENSE FORCES STAFF.

SIGINT OF ALL TYPES INCLUDING DEPLOYMENT OF TEAMS IN WAR ZONES AS DANGEROUS AS YEMEN/SYRIA /IRAQ/AFGHANISTAN ETC

ANTI PIRACY EW OPS IN INDIAN OCEAN --INSURGENT LOCATION STRATEGIES AND TECHNIQUES SUCCESSFULLY APPLIED AND PRACTISED IN YEMEN/IRAQ/AFGHANISTAN/FATA AREAS
ELINT Digital Analysis and Exploitation
-    Analysis process for different objectives(e.g. MTI, rejection performance, integration periods, resolvable range, PRF), data cleaning, data reduction and extraction, signal examination and processing, signal characterisation, interpulse/intrapulse analysis, wideband analysis, pulse doppler analysis, scan analysis, EW analysis, statistical/stability analysis using software tools, e.g. MARTES, ASPEN, search techniques based on airborne/land/ship platforms, PRF selection algorithm.

Countersurveillance @ mail.com
Security . logistics@ g mail.com

ELINT Operationalisation
-    Sensor platforms location considerations, sensor configurations, updating and maintaining emitter

ISBN-13: 978-1514684726 FOR FREE COLOURED ONE PAGE
ADVERTISEMENTS E MAIL US ON Transoxiana@mail.com
ISBN-10: 1514684721

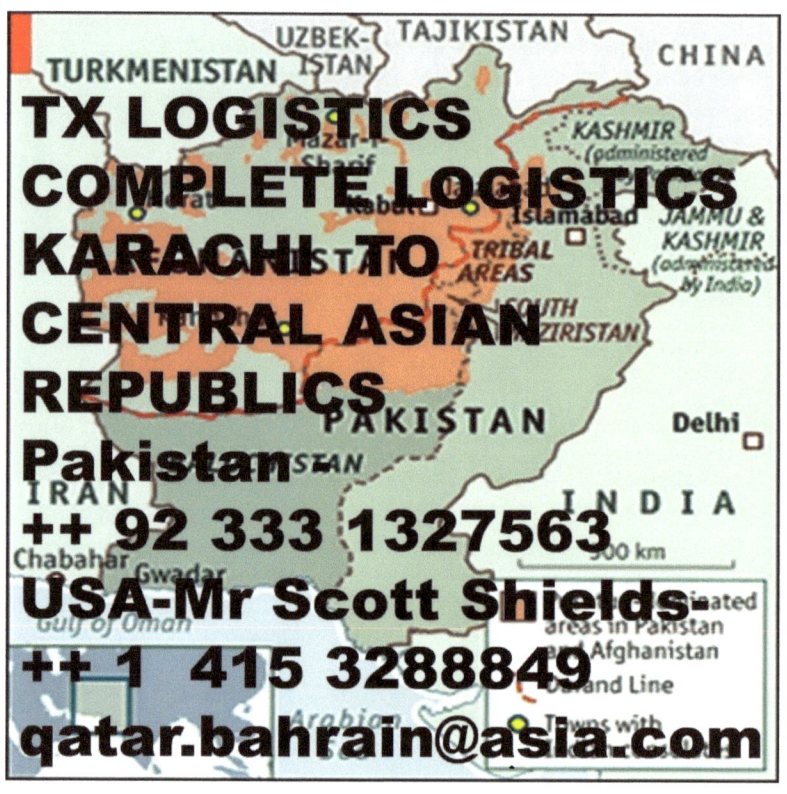

TX LOGISTICS
COMPLETE LOGISTICS
KARACHI TO
CENTRAL ASIAN
REPUBLICS
Pakistan
++ 92 333 1327563
USA-Mr Scott Shields
++ 1 415 3288849
qatar.bahrain@asia.com

FINAL WORKSHOP WITH SNC LAVALIN CANADA FOR CASA 1000 SURVEY IN AFGHANISTAN.
In the photograph , Phd Environment , Head of Environmental Engineering Department of SNC Lavalin Canada

WE SPECIALISE IN ENVIRONMENT AND SOCIAL IMPACT ASSESSMENT STUDIES WORLDWIDE
Security.logistics@gmail.com
CAN WORK IN ALL MIDDLE EAST/AFRICA/WORLDWIDE

ISBN-13: 978-1514684726 FOR FREE COLOURED ONE PAGE ADVERTISEMENTS E MAIL US ON Transoxiana@mail.com
ISBN-10: 1514684721

ANDERSON LLOYD
International Ltd.

Date: 25th August 2010.

Ref: Authorised Representative for Anderson Lloyd International Ltd -Major Agha H Amin (Retired).

I am pleased to confirm that Anderson Lloyd International Ltd have secured the services in Afghanistan of Major Agha H Amin (Retired). The Major will have full rights to introduce clients to Anderson Lloyd International Ltd and we are very happy to have secured this arrangement.

I can confirm that the Major will be able to liaise between clients in Afghanistan and Anderson Lloyd International Ltd; the leading brokers for all classes of insurance in Afghanistan. Anderson Lloyd International Ltd deal with Lloyds of London as well as select American insurance companies to provide our clients with the right cover at the right price.

Anderson Lloyd International Ltd deals with some of the largest companies operating in Afghanistan and has an excellent reputation in the insurance market.

Lloyds of London have an excellent reputation and a long history and we have an excellent relationship with many Lloyds Brokers and Underwriting Syndicates.

I trust that this letter will assist you in dealing with the Major and I am happy to answer any questions that you may have.

Anderson Lloyd International Ltd has offices in Kuwait and the UK and has dealt in the insurance business for many years.

Best regards,

Michael J Ellery,
Director,
Anderson Lloyd International Ltd.

P.O. Box 679, Yarmouk, Kuwait, 72657
Courier Address : Office 7, Bldg. 3, Kuwait Free Trade Zone, Shuwaikh, Kuwait
Tel.: +965 4610081 - Fax : +965 4610085 E-mail: office@andersonlloydintl.com www.andersonlloydintl.com

WITH MR MOSER THE TOP LEVEL EXPERT OF CONCRETE PAVERS IN THE WORLD DURING CONSULTATION OF PAVING STRATEGY FOR CONCRETE PAVING OF NEW ISLAMABAD INYERNATIONAL AIRPORT WHILE PERFORMING AS CONSULTANT OF HUSNAIN COTEX LAGAN UK JV FOR NEW ISLAMABAD INTERNATIONAL AIRPORT APRIL 2010

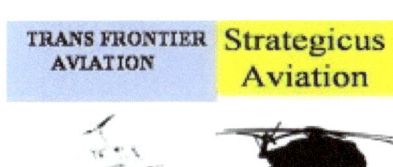

ISBN-13: 978-1514684726 FOR FREE COLOURED ONE PAGE ADVERTISEMENTS E MAIL US ON Transoxiana@mail.com ISBN-10: 1514684721

TRANSOXIANA AVIATION (TX AVIATION)

GRAND MAGIC GS 750 – FOUR SEATER

TX AVIATION IS SOLE DEALER FOR PAKISTAN AFGHANISTAN AND CAN ALSO PROVIDE WORLDWIDE INCLUDING UAE , CENTRAL ASIA ETC

**WE DO PILING AND
BORING WORKS
WORLDWIDE**

**FOR ANY WORK
INQUIRIES. GOOD
FEES WILL BE PAID TO
CONSULTANTS ALSO
PLEASE CONTACT
US ON
security.logistics@gmail.com**

**We Want Sales agents
on commission
basis worldwide
Contact us on:--
security.logistics@gmail.com**

WORLDS BEST TWO AND FOUR SEATER AURCRAFTS

ISBN-13: 978-1514684726 FOR FREE COLOURED ONE PAGE
ADVERTISEMENTS E MAIL US ON Transoxiana@mail.com
ISBN-10: 1514684721

IBIS AIRCRAFT S.A. COMPANY
Light and Experimental Aircraft Manufacturer

CERTIFY

That **Mr. Agha Shehryar** is authorized representative for marketing for IBIS AIRCRAFT S.A. in **PAKISTAN** and **AFGHANISTAN**.

Mr. Agha Shehryar is authorized for **IBIS AIRCRAFT S.A.** in **PAKISTAN** and **AFGHANISTAN** for the development of activities and commitments as an authorized, sole and exclusive representative for marketing of our aircrafts.
Contact details are listed below and are also available on the Ibis Aircraft website at:
www.ibis-aircraft.com

Complete Company Name: TRANSOXIANA
Contact: Agha Shehryar
City: Karachi
Country: Pakistan
Office Address: 20 C, Shahbaz Commercial Lane, Khayaban i Shahbaz, Phase Six, DHA, Karachi
Zip Code: Karachi
Airfield: Karachi
Zip Code: Karachi
Phones: + 92 331 8063998
Fax:
Web page:
Mobile: + 82 308 270 1926
Email: security.logistics@gmail.com
Skype:

In proof of this certification is issued in Cali, Colombia, South America, in the 9th day of April 2012.

Mario Sanchez
General Manager
IBIS AIRCRAFT S.A.
www.ibis-aircraft.com
Cali, Colombia, South America
Calle 13 A No. 100 – 35
Tel: 57 (2) – 6 81 44 33
Cel: 57 (2) – 314 7 92 54 17

IBIS AIRCRAFT S.A.
NIT. 800.206.844 - 7

Calle 13 A No. 100 - 35
Cali - Colombia - South America
Tel: 57 (2) – 6 81 44 33
Cel: 57 (2) – 314 7 92 54 17
www.ibis-aircraft.com
ibis@ibis-aircraft.com

ISBN-13: 978-1514684726 FOR FREE COLOURED ONE PAGE ADVERTISEMENTS E MAIL US ON Transoxiana@mail.com
ISBN-10: 1514684721

COMPANY PROFILE
YAQUBI BOATS

ISBN-13: 978-1514684726 FOR FREE COLOURED ONE PAGE
ADVERTISEMENTS E MAIL US ON Transoxiana@mail.com
ISBN-10: 1514684721

Yaqoobi Boats is a builder of quality boats in wood and fibreglass for work, fishing and pleasure. Our boats can be found sailing the seas around the Asian subcontinent.

Yaqoobi Boats has the capability to build a wide range of boat types. We have at our disposal a vast pool of skilled manpower possessing technical expertise and experience in all areas of wooden and fibreglass boat construction. Adapting to the demands

ISBN-13: 978-1514684726 FOR FREE COLOURED ONE PAGE ADVERTISEMENTS E MAIL US ON Transoxiana@mail.com
ISBN-10: 1514684721

of present day business, we have re-organised ourselves to work under minimal overheads and where suitable, take advantage of available existing facilities that meet our construction requirements. We thereby run a flexible operation and are not confined to building boats at Gwadar Pakistan alone. Your boat is individually built by our own skilled work team and our usual standard of workmanship and personal commitment is assured.

ISBN-13: 978-1514684726 FOR FREE COLOURED ONE PAGE ADVERTISEMENTS E MAIL US ON Transoxiana@mail.com ISBN-10: 1514684721

Take advantage of the lower cost of skilled manpower in Asia and get your boat built by us. Choose one of the standard boats shown on the accompanying webpages, or have their layouts customized to suit your own requirements. Boats can be supplied bare shell or complete. Owners/designers are also invited to discuss having their own design custom-built by us. Furnish study prints and bill of materials of your design for a quote. Facilities and skilled

ISBN-13: 978-1514684726 FOR FREE COLOURED ONE PAGE ADVERTISEMENTS E MAIL US ON Transoxiana@mail.com
ISBN-10: 1514684721

manpower can be organized for having your boat built under your personal instructions.

Production boatbuilders can explore the possibility of getting hulls and other parts of their series produced boats hand lay-up moulded by us in moulds and materials supplied either by them or us. Moulding of FRP parts for other applications as per your design is also undertaken. We are in close liaison with product development centres of

ISBN-13: 978-1514684726 FOR FREE COLOURED ONE PAGE ADVERTISEMENTS E MAIL US ON Transoxiana@mail.com ISBN-10: 1514684721

major wooden/glassfibre manufacturing companies and other institutions.

You are invited to contact us for liaison work and other marine related services in the region. Contact from boat designers and other boat-builders with the aim of pooling together resources and offering the customer a wider range of products and services is also welcome.

ISBN-13: 978-1514684726 FOR FREE COLOURED ONE PAGE ADVERTISEMENTS E MAIL US ON Transoxiana@mail.com ISBN-10: 1514684721

Cost of construction of a boat is exorbitantly high in Iran, UAE and Persian Gulf states.

ISBN-13: 978-1514684726 FOR FREE COLOURED ONE PAGE ADVERTISEMENTS E MAIL US ON Transoxiana@mail.com
ISBN-10: 1514684721

YAQUBI BOATS ARE IN HIGH DEMAND IN ALL INDIAN OCEAN STATES.

CONTACT DETAILS:--

makran@asia.com

Transoxiana@mail.com

UAE - ++ 9715 65650284

++9715 64696702

PAKISTAN AND AFGHANISTAN

++ 92 333 1327563

++ 92 315 5399897

SKYPE- strategicus7

ISBN-13: 978-1514684726 FOR FREE COLOURED ONE PAGE ADVERTISEMENTS E MAIL US ON Transoxiana@mail.com
ISBN-10: 1514684721

WORLDS BEST INVESTMENT

DAMAC PROPERTIES

'Villa Options', these are 'Villas' in the largest golf/park community of Asia spanning over '42 Million Square Feet / 964 Acres', known by the name of 'Akoya' BY DAMAC. The location is off the 'Umm Sequim' road and is 10 Minutes drive away from the 'Mall of Emirates', near 'Arabian Ranches'.

Villa (SD & Independent) varies from AED 3.4 Million to AED 110 Million. Special Payment plan offer is till Eid only.

Contact Transoxiana and get a complete briefing about WORLDS BEST INVESTMENT

Transoxiana@mail.com

UAE - ++ 9715 65650284   ++9715 64696702

ISBN-13: 978-1514684726 FOR FREE COLOURED ONE PAGE ADVERTISEMENTS E MAIL US ON Transoxiana@mail.com ISBN-10: 1514684721

PAKISTAN AND AFGHANISTAN   ++ 92 333 1327563

++ 92 315 5399897

SKYPE- strategicus7

<u>The Clubhouse Image</u>

One of the biggest and the most prestigious golf communities of ASIA & EUROPE.

Below are onsite images of AKOYA by DAMAC .

The construction is in full swing by AL NABOODAH CONSTRUCTION (Civil Contractors).

ISBN-13: 978-1514684726 FOR FREE COLOURED ONE PAGE ADVERTISEMENTS E MAIL US ON Transoxiana@mail.com
ISBN-10: 1514684721

ISBN-13: 978-1514684726 FOR FREE COLOURED ONE PAGE
ADVERTISEMENTS E MAIL US ON Transoxiana@mail.com
ISBN-10: 1514684721

ISBN-13: 978-1514684726 FOR FREE COLOURED ONE PAGE
ADVERTISEMENTS E MAIL US ON Transoxiana@mail.com
ISBN-10: 1514684721

WHATS WRONG WITH DUBAI AIRPORT

ISBN-13: 978-1514684726 FOR FREE COLOURED ONE PAGE
ADVERTISEMENTS E MAIL US ON Transoxiana@mail.com
ISBN-10: 1514684721

It was a rude shock waiting for my flight of SHAHEEN AIRLINES PAKISTAN , world's most unprofessional and disorganized airline.

I had to wait for my flight for nine hours and imagine these chairs on which I had to literally cramp my muscles and damage my health and wellbeing.

ISBN-13: 978-1514684726 FOR FREE COLOURED ONE PAGE ADVERTISEMENTS E MAIL US ON Transoxiana@mail.com
ISBN-10: 1514684721

SOMETHING IS SERIOUSLY WRONG WITH DUBAI AIRPORT !

ISBN-13: 978-1514684726 FOR FREE COLOURED ONE PAGE ADVERTISEMENTS E MAIL US ON Transoxiana@mail.com
ISBN-10: 1514684721

ISBN-13: 978-1514684726 FOR FREE COLOURED ONE PAGE
ADVERTISEMENTS E MAIL US ON Transoxiana@mail.com
ISBN-10: 1514684721

ISBN-13: 978-1514684726 FOR FREE COLOURED ONE PAGE
ADVERTISEMENTS E MAIL US ON Transoxiana@mail.com
ISBN-10: 1514684721

ISBN-13: 978-1514684726 FOR FREE COLOURED ONE PAGE
ADVERTISEMENTS E MAIL US ON Transoxiana@mail.com
ISBN-10: 1514684721